50 Fresh & Flavorful Salad Dressings

By: Kelly Johnson

Table of Contents

- Classic Vinaigrette
- Balsamic Vinaigrette
- Lemon Herb Dressing
- Honey Mustard Dressing
- Ranch Dressing
- Blue Cheese Dressing
- Caesar Dressing
- Green Goddess Dressing
- Italian Dressing
- Thousand Island Dressing
- Sesame Ginger Dressing
- Tahini Dressing
- Avocado Lime Dressing
- Raspberry Vinaigrette
- Greek Dressing
- Orange Poppy Seed Dressing
- Cilantro Lime Dressing
- Miso Dressing
- Yogurt Dill Dressing
- Cucumber Mint Dressing
- Spicy Peanut Dressing
- Mustard Vinaigrette
- Apple Cider Vinaigrette
- Maple Dijon Dressing
- Roasted Garlic Dressing
- Shallot Vinaigrette
- Lemon Poppy Seed Dressing
- Cilantro Mint Dressing
- Coconut Lime Dressing
- Basil Pesto Dressing
- Tomato Basil Dressing
- Creamy Parmesan Dressing
- Sesame Soy Dressing
- Blackberry Vinaigrette
- Mango Lime Dressing

- Spicy Sriracha Dressing
- Honey Lime Dressing
- Turmeric Ginger Dressing
- Curry Yogurt Dressing
- Dill Cucumber Dressing
- Carrot Ginger Dressing
- Lemon Garlic Dressing
- Spicy Cilantro Dressing
- Roasted Red Pepper Dressing
- White Balsamic Vinaigrette
- Tamarind Dressing
- Fennel Orange Dressing
- Strawberry Basil Dressing
- Avocado Cilantro Dressing
- Lime Chili Dressing

Classic Vinaigrette

Ingredients:

- 3 tablespoons olive oil
- 1 tablespoon red wine vinegar
- 1 teaspoon Dijon mustard
- 1 clove garlic, minced
- Salt and pepper, to taste

Instructions:

1. In a small bowl, whisk together the red wine vinegar, Dijon mustard, and minced garlic.
2. Slowly drizzle in the olive oil while continuing to whisk until emulsified.
3. Season with salt and pepper to taste.

Balsamic Vinaigrette

Ingredients:

- 3 tablespoons olive oil
- 1 tablespoon balsamic vinegar
- 1 teaspoon honey
- 1 teaspoon Dijon mustard
- Salt and pepper, to taste

Instructions:

1. In a small bowl, combine balsamic vinegar, honey, and Dijon mustard.
2. Slowly whisk in the olive oil until the dressing is well combined.
3. Season with salt and pepper to taste.

Lemon Herb Dressing

Ingredients:

- 3 tablespoons olive oil
- 1 tablespoon fresh lemon juice
- 1 teaspoon honey
- 1 teaspoon chopped fresh herbs (parsley, thyme, or basil)
- Salt and pepper, to taste

Instructions:

1. In a small bowl, whisk together lemon juice, honey, and chopped herbs.
2. Gradually add olive oil, whisking until emulsified.
3. Season with salt and pepper to taste.

Honey Mustard Dressing

Ingredients:

- 2 tablespoons Dijon mustard
- 2 tablespoons honey
- 2 tablespoons apple cider vinegar
- 1/4 cup olive oil
- Salt and pepper, to taste

Instructions:

1. In a bowl, whisk together Dijon mustard, honey, and apple cider vinegar.
2. Slowly add olive oil, whisking until well blended.
3. Season with salt and pepper to taste.

Ranch Dressing

Ingredients:

- 1/2 cup mayonnaise
- 1/2 cup sour cream
- 1/4 cup buttermilk
- 1 clove garlic, minced
- 1 teaspoon dried dill
- 1 teaspoon dried parsley
- 1 teaspoon onion powder
- Salt and pepper, to taste

Instructions:

1. In a bowl, combine mayonnaise, sour cream, and buttermilk.
2. Stir in minced garlic, dill, parsley, and onion powder.
3. Season with salt and pepper to taste. Chill before serving.

Blue Cheese Dressing

Ingredients:

- 1/2 cup mayonnaise
- 1/4 cup sour cream
- 1/4 cup buttermilk
- 1/4 cup crumbled blue cheese
- 1 teaspoon lemon juice
- Salt and pepper, to taste

Instructions:

1. In a bowl, mix mayonnaise, sour cream, and buttermilk.
2. Stir in crumbled blue cheese and lemon juice.
3. Season with salt and pepper to taste. Refrigerate before serving.

Caesar Dressing

Ingredients:

- 1/2 cup mayonnaise
- 2 tablespoons lemon juice
- 1 teaspoon Dijon mustard
- 1 clove garlic, minced
- 1/4 cup grated Parmesan cheese
- 2 anchovy fillets, minced (optional)
- Salt and pepper, to taste

Instructions:

1. In a bowl, combine mayonnaise, lemon juice, Dijon mustard, and minced garlic.
2. Stir in Parmesan cheese and anchovy fillets (if using).
3. Season with salt and pepper to taste.

Green Goddess Dressing

Ingredients:

- 1/2 cup mayonnaise
- 1/4 cup sour cream
- 2 tablespoons lemon juice
- 1 clove garlic, minced
- 2 tablespoons chopped fresh parsley
- 1 tablespoon chopped fresh chives
- 1 tablespoon chopped tarragon
- Salt and pepper, to taste

Instructions:

1. In a bowl, mix mayonnaise, sour cream, and lemon juice.
2. Add minced garlic, parsley, chives, and tarragon.
3. Season with salt and pepper to taste. Chill before serving.

Italian Dressing

Ingredients:

- 1/2 cup olive oil
- 1/4 cup white wine vinegar
- 1 teaspoon dried oregano
- 1 teaspoon dried basil
- 1 clove garlic, minced
- 1 teaspoon Dijon mustard
- Salt and pepper, to taste

Instructions:

1. In a bowl, whisk together white wine vinegar, oregano, basil, minced garlic, and Dijon mustard.
2. Gradually add olive oil, whisking until emulsified.
3. Season with salt and pepper to taste.

Thousand Island Dressing

Ingredients:

- 1/2 cup mayonnaise
- 2 tablespoons ketchup
- 1 tablespoon sweet pickle relish
- 1 teaspoon white vinegar
- 1 teaspoon sugar
- Salt and pepper, to taste

Instructions:

1. In a bowl, combine mayonnaise, ketchup, sweet pickle relish, white vinegar, and sugar.
2. Mix well and season with salt and pepper to taste.

Sesame Ginger Dressing

Ingredients:

- 1/4 cup soy sauce
- 2 tablespoons rice vinegar
- 1 tablespoon sesame oil
- 1 tablespoon grated ginger
- 1 clove garlic, minced
- 1 teaspoon honey
- 1 tablespoon vegetable oil

Instructions:

1. In a bowl, whisk together soy sauce, rice vinegar, sesame oil, grated ginger, minced garlic, and honey.
2. Slowly add vegetable oil while whisking until the dressing is well combined.

Tahini Dressing

Ingredients:

- 1/4 cup tahini
- 2 tablespoons lemon juice
- 1 clove garlic, minced
- 2 tablespoons water
- Salt and pepper, to taste

Instructions:

1. In a bowl, whisk together tahini, lemon juice, and minced garlic.
2. Gradually add water until the dressing reaches your desired consistency.
3. Season with salt and pepper to taste.

Avocado Lime Dressing

Ingredients:

- 1 ripe avocado
- 2 tablespoons lime juice
- 2 tablespoons olive oil
- 1 clove garlic, minced
- Salt and pepper, to taste

Instructions:

1. In a blender, combine avocado, lime juice, olive oil, and minced garlic.
2. Blend until smooth and season with salt and pepper to taste.

Raspberry Vinaigrette

Ingredients:

- 1/4 cup fresh raspberries
- 2 tablespoons red wine vinegar
- 1 teaspoon honey
- 1/4 cup olive oil
- Salt and pepper, to taste

Instructions:

1. In a blender, puree raspberries with red wine vinegar and honey.
2. Slowly drizzle in olive oil while blending until smooth.
3. Season with salt and pepper to taste.

Greek Dressing

Ingredients:

- 1/4 cup olive oil
- 2 tablespoons red wine vinegar
- 1 clove garlic, minced
- 1 teaspoon dried oregano
- 1/4 teaspoon salt
- Black pepper, to taste

Instructions:

1. In a bowl, whisk together red wine vinegar, minced garlic, oregano, salt, and black pepper.
2. Slowly add olive oil while whisking until the dressing is emulsified.

Orange Poppy Seed Dressing

Ingredients:

- 1/4 cup orange juice
- 2 tablespoons apple cider vinegar
- 1 tablespoon honey
- 1 teaspoon poppy seeds
- 1/4 cup olive oil
- Salt and pepper, to taste

Instructions:

1. In a bowl, whisk together orange juice, apple cider vinegar, honey, and poppy seeds.
2. Slowly add olive oil while whisking until the dressing is well combined.
3. Season with salt and pepper to taste.

Cilantro Lime Dressing

Ingredients:

- 1/2 cup fresh cilantro leaves
- 2 tablespoons lime juice
- 1 clove garlic, minced
- 1/4 cup olive oil
- Salt and pepper, to taste

Instructions:

1. In a blender, combine cilantro, lime juice, minced garlic, and olive oil.
2. Blend until smooth and season with salt and pepper to taste.

Miso Dressing

Ingredients:

- 2 tablespoons white miso paste
- 2 tablespoons rice vinegar
- 1 tablespoon sesame oil
- 1 tablespoon soy sauce
- 1 tablespoon water
- 1 teaspoon honey

Instructions:

1. In a bowl, whisk together miso paste, rice vinegar, sesame oil, soy sauce, water, and honey until smooth.

Yogurt Dill Dressing

Ingredients:

- 1/2 cup plain yogurt
- 1 tablespoon fresh dill, chopped
- 1 tablespoon lemon juice
- 1 clove garlic, minced
- Salt and pepper, to taste

Instructions:

1. In a bowl, combine yogurt, dill, lemon juice, and minced garlic.
2. Mix well and season with salt and pepper to taste.

Cucumber Mint Dressing

Ingredients:

- 1/2 cup cucumber, peeled and grated
- 2 tablespoons fresh mint, chopped
- 1/4 cup plain yogurt
- 1 tablespoon lemon juice
- Salt and pepper, to taste

Instructions:

1. In a bowl, mix cucumber, mint, yogurt, and lemon juice.
2. Season with salt and pepper to taste.

Spicy Peanut Dressing

Ingredients:

- 1/4 cup peanut butter
- 2 tablespoons soy sauce
- 1 tablespoon rice vinegar
- 1 tablespoon honey
- 1 teaspoon chili paste
- 2 tablespoons water

Instructions:

1. In a bowl, whisk together peanut butter, soy sauce, rice vinegar, honey, chili paste, and water until smooth.

Mustard Vinaigrette

Ingredients:

- 1 tablespoon Dijon mustard
- 2 tablespoons red wine vinegar
- 1/4 cup olive oil
- Salt and pepper, to taste

Instructions:

1. In a bowl, whisk together Dijon mustard and red wine vinegar.
2. Slowly add olive oil while whisking until emulsified.
3. Season with salt and pepper to taste.

Apple Cider Vinaigrette

Ingredients:

- 1/4 cup apple cider vinegar
- 1 tablespoon honey
- 1/2 teaspoon Dijon mustard
- 1/4 cup olive oil
- Salt and pepper, to taste

Instructions:

1. In a bowl, whisk together apple cider vinegar, honey, and Dijon mustard.
2. Slowly add olive oil while whisking until the dressing is well combined.
3. Season with salt and pepper to taste.

Maple Dijon Dressing

Ingredients:

- 2 tablespoons maple syrup
- 1 tablespoon Dijon mustard
- 1 tablespoon apple cider vinegar
- 1/4 cup olive oil
- Salt and pepper, to taste

Instructions:

1. In a bowl, whisk together maple syrup, Dijon mustard, and apple cider vinegar.
2. Slowly add olive oil while whisking until emulsified.
3. Season with salt and pepper to taste.

Roasted Garlic Dressing

Ingredients:

- 1 head garlic, roasted
- 2 tablespoons lemon juice
- 1/4 cup olive oil
- Salt and pepper, to taste

Instructions:

1. Squeeze the roasted garlic cloves into a bowl.
2. Add lemon juice and mash the garlic until smooth.
3. Slowly add olive oil while whisking until the dressing is well combined.
4. Season with salt and pepper to taste.

Shallot Vinaigrette

Ingredients:

- 1 shallot, finely minced
- 2 tablespoons red wine vinegar
- 1/2 teaspoon Dijon mustard
- 1/4 cup olive oil
- Salt and pepper, to taste

Instructions:

1. In a bowl, combine minced shallot, red wine vinegar, and Dijon mustard.
2. Slowly add olive oil while whisking until emulsified.
3. Season with salt and pepper to taste.

Lemon Poppy Seed Dressing

Ingredients:

- 1/4 cup lemon juice
- 2 tablespoons honey
- 1 teaspoon poppy seeds
- 1/4 cup olive oil
- Salt and pepper, to taste

Instructions:

1. In a bowl, whisk together lemon juice, honey, and poppy seeds.
2. Slowly add olive oil while whisking until the dressing is well combined.
3. Season with salt and pepper to taste.

Cilantro Mint Dressing

Ingredients:

- 1/2 cup fresh cilantro
- 1/4 cup fresh mint
- 2 tablespoons lime juice
- 2 tablespoons olive oil
- 1 tablespoon honey
- Salt and pepper, to taste

Instructions:

1. Blend cilantro, mint, lime juice, olive oil, and honey until smooth.
2. Season with salt and pepper to taste.

Coconut Lime Dressing

Ingredients:

- 1/4 cup coconut milk
- 2 tablespoons lime juice
- 1 tablespoon olive oil
- 1 teaspoon honey
- Salt and pepper, to taste

Instructions:

1. Whisk together coconut milk, lime juice, olive oil, and honey.
2. Season with salt and pepper to taste.

Basil Pesto Dressing

Ingredients:

- 1/2 cup fresh basil
- 2 tablespoons pine nuts
- 2 tablespoons olive oil
- 1 tablespoon lemon juice
- 1 garlic clove
- Salt and pepper, to taste

Instructions:

1. Blend basil, pine nuts, olive oil, lemon juice, and garlic until smooth.
2. Season with salt and pepper to taste.

Tomato Basil Dressing

Ingredients:

- 1/2 cup cherry tomatoes, chopped
- 2 tablespoons fresh basil, chopped
- 2 tablespoons olive oil
- 1 tablespoon balsamic vinegar
- Salt and pepper, to taste

Instructions:

1. Blend cherry tomatoes, basil, olive oil, and balsamic vinegar until smooth.
2. Season with salt and pepper to taste.

Creamy Parmesan Dressing

Ingredients:

- 1/4 cup grated Parmesan cheese
- 1/4 cup mayonnaise
- 2 tablespoons lemon juice
- 1 tablespoon olive oil
- 1 garlic clove, minced
- Salt and pepper, to taste

Instructions:

1. Whisk together Parmesan cheese, mayonnaise, lemon juice, olive oil, and garlic.
2. Season with salt and pepper to taste.

Sesame Soy Dressing

Ingredients:

- 2 tablespoons soy sauce
- 1 tablespoon sesame oil
- 1 tablespoon rice vinegar
- 1 teaspoon honey
- 1/2 teaspoon grated ginger

Instructions:

1. Whisk together soy sauce, sesame oil, rice vinegar, honey, and grated ginger.

Blackberry Vinaigrette

Ingredients:

- 1/2 cup blackberries
- 2 tablespoons balsamic vinegar
- 1 tablespoon olive oil
- 1 teaspoon honey
- Salt and pepper, to taste

Instructions:

1. Blend blackberries, balsamic vinegar, olive oil, and honey until smooth.
2. Season with salt and pepper to taste.

Mango Lime Dressing

Ingredients:

- 1/2 cup ripe mango, chopped
- 2 tablespoons lime juice
- 1 tablespoon olive oil
- 1 teaspoon honey
- Salt and pepper, to taste

Instructions:

1. Blend mango, lime juice, olive oil, and honey until smooth.
2. Season with salt and pepper to taste.

Spicy Sriracha Dressing

Ingredients:

- 2 tablespoons Sriracha sauce
- 2 tablespoons mayonnaise
- 1 tablespoon lime juice
- 1 teaspoon honey
- Salt, to taste

Instructions:

1. Whisk together Sriracha, mayonnaise, lime juice, and honey.
2. Season with salt to taste.

Honey Lime Dressing

Ingredients:

- 2 tablespoons honey
- 2 tablespoons lime juice
- 1 tablespoon olive oil
- 1/2 teaspoon lime zest
- Salt and pepper, to taste

Instructions:

1. In a bowl, whisk together honey, lime juice, olive oil, and lime zest.
2. Season with salt and pepper to taste.

Turmeric Ginger Dressing

Ingredients:

- 1 tablespoon turmeric powder
- 1 tablespoon grated ginger
- 2 tablespoons lemon juice
- 2 tablespoons olive oil
- 1 tablespoon honey
- Salt and pepper, to taste

Instructions:

1. In a bowl, mix turmeric, ginger, lemon juice, olive oil, and honey until well combined.
2. Season with salt and pepper to taste.

Curry Yogurt Dressing

Ingredients:

- 1/4 cup plain yogurt
- 1 tablespoon curry powder
- 1 tablespoon lemon juice
- 1 tablespoon olive oil
- Salt and pepper, to taste

Instructions:

1. In a bowl, whisk together yogurt, curry powder, lemon juice, and olive oil.
2. Season with salt and pepper to taste.

Dill Cucumber Dressing

Ingredients:

- 1/2 cup cucumber, diced
- 2 tablespoons fresh dill, chopped
- 1/4 cup Greek yogurt
- 1 tablespoon lemon juice
- Salt and pepper, to taste

Instructions:

1. Blend cucumber, dill, yogurt, and lemon juice until smooth.
2. Season with salt and pepper to taste.

Carrot Ginger Dressing

Ingredients:

- 1/2 cup carrots, chopped
- 1 tablespoon grated ginger
- 2 tablespoons rice vinegar
- 1 tablespoon sesame oil
- 1 tablespoon honey

Instructions:

1. Blend carrots, ginger, rice vinegar, sesame oil, and honey until smooth.

Lemon Garlic Dressing

Ingredients:

- 2 tablespoons lemon juice
- 1 clove garlic, minced
- 2 tablespoons olive oil
- 1 teaspoon Dijon mustard
- Salt and pepper, to taste

Instructions:

1. In a bowl, whisk together lemon juice, garlic, olive oil, and Dijon mustard.
2. Season with salt and pepper to taste.

Spicy Cilantro Dressing

Ingredients:

- 1/2 cup fresh cilantro, chopped
- 1 jalapeño, seeded and chopped
- 2 tablespoons lime juice
- 1 tablespoon olive oil
- Salt and pepper, to taste

Instructions:

1. Blend cilantro, jalapeño, lime juice, and olive oil until smooth.
2. Season with salt and pepper to taste.

Roasted Red Pepper Dressing

Ingredients:

- 1/2 cup roasted red peppers, chopped
- 2 tablespoons balsamic vinegar
- 1 tablespoon olive oil
- 1 clove garlic, minced
- Salt and pepper, to taste

Instructions:

1. Blend roasted red peppers, balsamic vinegar, olive oil, and garlic until smooth.
2. Season with salt and pepper to taste.

White Balsamic Vinaigrette

Ingredients:

- 2 tablespoons white balsamic vinegar
- 1 tablespoon honey
- 2 tablespoons olive oil
- Salt and pepper, to taste

Instructions:

1. In a bowl, whisk together white balsamic vinegar, honey, and olive oil.
2. Season with salt and pepper to taste.

Tamarind Dressing

Ingredients:

- 2 tablespoons tamarind paste
- 1 tablespoon honey
- 2 tablespoons olive oil
- 1 tablespoon lime juice
- Salt and pepper, to taste

Instructions:

1. In a bowl, whisk together tamarind paste, honey, olive oil, and lime juice.
2. Season with salt and pepper to taste.

Fennel Orange Dressing

Ingredients:

- 1/2 cup fresh orange juice
- 1 tablespoon fennel seeds, toasted and ground
- 2 tablespoons olive oil
- 1 teaspoon honey
- Salt and pepper, to taste

Instructions:

1. In a bowl, whisk together orange juice, ground fennel seeds, olive oil, and honey.
2. Season with salt and pepper to taste.

Strawberry Basil Dressing

Ingredients:

- 1/2 cup fresh strawberries, chopped
- 2 tablespoons fresh basil, chopped
- 2 tablespoons balsamic vinegar
- 1 tablespoon olive oil
- Salt and pepper, to taste

Instructions:

1. Blend strawberries, basil, balsamic vinegar, and olive oil until smooth.
2. Season with salt and pepper to taste.

Avocado Cilantro Dressing

Ingredients:

- 1 avocado, peeled and pitted
- 1/2 cup fresh cilantro, chopped
- 2 tablespoons lime juice
- 1 tablespoon olive oil
- Salt and pepper, to taste

Instructions:

1. Blend avocado, cilantro, lime juice, and olive oil until smooth.
2. Season with salt and pepper to taste.

Lime Chili Dressing

Ingredients:

- 2 tablespoons lime juice
- 1 teaspoon chili powder
- 2 tablespoons olive oil
- 1 tablespoon honey
- Salt and pepper, to taste

Instructions:

1. In a bowl, whisk together lime juice, chili powder, olive oil, and honey.
2. Season with salt and pepper to taste.